MANHATTAN AS A SECOND LANGUAGE

This House That Rocks with Every Truck on the Road
Letters from the Promise Land, Alaska
Pin Money
The Book of Common People: Poems in a Dime Store Sack
The Clackamas
Who's That Pushy Bitch?
Alaska, A Novel

Manhattan as a Second Language

And Other Poems

JANA HARRIS

1817

Harper & Row, Publishers, San Francisco

Cambridge, Hagerstown, New York, Philadelphia
London, Mexico City, São Paulo, Sydney

MANHATTAN AS A SECOND LANGUAGE *And Other Poems.* Copyright ©1982 by Jana Harris. All rights reserved. Printed in the United States of America. No part of this book may be used or reproduced in any manner whatsoever without written permission except in the case of brief quotations embodied in critical articles and reviews. For information address Harper & Row, Publishers, Inc., 10 East 53rd Street, New York, NY 10022. Published simultaneously in Canada by Fitzhenry & Whiteside, Limited, Toronto.

FIRST EDITION

Designer: Jim Mennick

Library of Congress Cataloging in Publication Data

Harris, Jana.
  Manhattan as a second language and other poems.

  I. Title.
PS3558.A6462M3   1982   811'.54   81-47851
ISBN 0-06-250383-9   AACR2

82 83 84 85 86   10 9 8 7 6 5 4 3 2 1

Talent and luck aside, the literary careers of women are made up of hard work, a resilience to rejection, a devotion to personal vision, and the often bottomless need for faith and support from friends.

To those people in my life to whom this book truly belongs:

Mary Mackey and Valerie Miner, Carol Murray,
Mark Bothwell, Marie Dern and Carl Dern

Contents

Acknowledgments

The author gratefully acknowledges the editors and publishers of the following publications, in which some of the poems in this book appeared:

BOOKS: *The 1978 Napa College Catalog; Anthology of the First Annual Women's Poetry Festival of San Francisco* (New World Press Collective); *Networks, An Anthology of San Francisco Bay Area Women Poets* (Vortex Editions); *The Clackamas* (The Smith); *This House that Rocks with Every Truck on the Road* (Jungle Garden Press); *Pin Money* (Jungle Garden Press); *19 + 1, An Anthology of San Francisco Poets* (Second Coming); *Calafia* (Y'Bird Books); *The Obsession: Reflections on the Tyranny of Slenderness*, Kim Chernin (Harper & Row).

BROADSIDES: *Letters from the Promise Land, Alaska* (Jungle Garden Press); *The Book of Common People: Poems in a Dime Store Sack* (Alameda County Neighborhood Arts Program); *Desperado* (Jungle Garden Press); *Angelica* (Jungle Garden Press).

MAGAZINES: *Beatitudes; California Living* (Sunday magazine section, *San Francisco Examiner and Chronicle*); *WPA 11; New Letters; The Nation; Bay Area Review of the Performing Arts; Ms. Magazine; Off Our Backs; Berkeley Poetry Review; East Bay Voice; Plexus; Quilt; Poetry Flash; Birthstone; Kosmos; Passage; Conditions.*

For their stories, their language, their bits and pieces, for their faith and support, their editorial assistance, their teaching, their camaraderie:

Jane Duncan, Ernest Landauer, Harry Smith, Alan Soldofsky, Richard Katz, Gloria Frym, Barbara Gravelle, Kate Ellis, Louise Bernikow, Beau Beausoleil, all the people at Cody's Books, Gary Traucht, Berkeley Civic Arts Commission, Alameda County Neighborhood Arts Program, Margo Laine, Dennis Gallagher, Sturm & Drang Design, Mary Kaczenski Brandon, Clive Matson, Marlys Mayfield, Rick and Edith Foster, David Ignatow, KPFA Radio, KSAN Radio, CETA, Jeannie Lum, Peti Taylor, Alie Smaalders, Al Young, Ishmael Reed, Carol Simone, Susan Suntree, Philip Suntree, The Bacchanal, Kay Boyle, Robert Creeley, Candy Hyde, Renee Lieberman, Don Cook, Marion Fay, Alta, Jane Ciabattari, A. D. Winans, Fred and Betty Berry, John Pearson, Maurice Kenny, Faye Kicknosway, Chris Hackett, Patricia Jones, Jane Ellis, Jon Ford, Jack Marshall, Carol Lee Sanchez, Marie Cantlon, Kathy Reigstad, Joanne Farness.

Manhattan as a Second Language

for Kate Ellis

in this new place
from a 12th-story window
she looks across black
smokestacked roofs
writing about Alaska

and the Aleut raven
guarding Spirit-of-the-Smoke-Hole,
thinks of going down
into the street
windows curtained

walleyed and blindpulled
not into the language of seabirds
but transistor radio nag rock
noise different from
her fisherman father

corn liquor drunk
and hollering like a gull
in a wind-topped spruce,
thinks of going down
into the street

into Puerto Rican style
"Be-bop-a-lula, she's my baby"
into   hey lady, what's your number
hey lady, I'm talkin to you,
things they wouldn't be saying

back home where everybody knew
her old man was one bad *hombre*,
thinks of going down
into the street
into the language

of rum-eyed men on
the Hotel Iroquois front stoop,
the womanlanguage, swolnbellied
years of beans and rice
on their thighs,

baby on a knee watching
the man eyes he will one day have,
thinks of Alaska
skyscrapers where cobaltcolored
glaciers and steep cliffs

ought to be,
thinks of them in the street
from the land of bougainvillea
and sugar cane, fields
they did not own, a homeland

like hers left behind
for work and Nueva York,
thinks of going down
into the street
into liquor slurred   *mira, mira*

no tengo, words
she has no meaning for,
thinks of how she might
write in a poem
that there ain't no luck

in them broomhandle-killing
that squirrel, carstunned and lost
from a tree in the park,
how she might make Manhattan
understand that sure as

humpbacked salmon run in June
that squirrel's soul'll find
its way inside a broomhandle,
clubbing those front-stoop men
the same way it got clubbed,

thinks of Alaska
thinks of going down
into the street
belonging to no one
like her homeland belongs

to no one with her own face on,
into   if your husband's a leg man
try our chicken parts,
into the manstare backtalk
and backglare of the others

exiled to this land of money
leafgold and applerot,
thinks of Alaska
and how she might tell
them in the street

about the Bering Sea
williwaw wind
blowing ice across Adak,
across the black dust
and volcano light through the fog,

thinks of Alaska
and not the slow-consonant
sharp-vowelled street radio DJ talk,
thinks of Sister MacElroy's
tundra radio ministry

Altar of the Air, "by the rivers
of Babylon"   *gringa, gringa*
"She's the gal in the red blue jeans,"
thinks of the feel
of their liquored streeteyes

upon her, thinks of the feel
of a half-pint bottle
their common language
in her hand
thinks about going down

into the street

(1978)

Tales

(1977–1980)

When Mama Came Here as a Gold Panner

when mama came here as a gold panner,
she climbed the Chilkoot pass
her long skirts trailin
through snow three feet high
and ice makin her snowblind,
fifty pound rucksack
baby under one arm
when mama came here as a gold panner,
said she was spread so thin
she felt like glass

spread so thin there was holes
in her pie dough, wildberry cobbler
she made'n sold to miners, while
by hand she washed their clothes
with lye soap she'd made by hand,
didn't work fast enough, the men
they'd slap her down back then
was what they did with women
was what they did with cows,
when mama came here as a gold panner,
said she was spread so thin
she felt like glass

like winter ice with the rations
eaten when Mama's hair turned
white as mine, I know
cause she cut'n knotted it into flowers
after doin miner's mendin,
pressed em in her Bible kept
between her sewing basket and darning egg
when mama came here as a gold panner,
said she was spread so thin
she felt like glass

thin as money when the gold run out,
turned her kitchen to a museum
and from all around people came
lookin at her pie pans
runnin fingers down
the hand-hewn shaft of her rollin pin,
but when she died
her kraut cutter'n butter paddle
got auctioned off like cattle,
who'd make history from a woman
who was all her life spread so thin

spread so thin there was holes
in her pie dough, frayed
like the miner's socks she mended,
like her broken kitchen window
spider cracks runnin to the sill
to the water-soaked and rotten window sash,
the hole where the hunter's bullet
winged the pane spider veined
like her upper thighs
when mama came here as a gold panner,
said she was spread so thin

spread so thin she felt like glass

The Last Voyage of the Eudora Dawn

Listening to loon squawk
echoing off the island rocks
and looking out her window
through a dead blackened eye,
lip stitched and cheekbone sunk in;
I always wondered, she said,
why fishin boats
got women's names
painted on their bows
like the salmon troller
Eudora Dawn
that my husband named for me.
I always wondered, she said
watching Icy Bay tide and boa kelp
batter the hull
rusted from running aground
in a Southeast Alaska blow.
Until last Sunday, she said,
helpin him make bullets
outta blastin caps'n gunpowder.
Gonna fill up our freezer
with elk wild game meat,
he said, and I said
wish you wouldn't stay out
so late at the Elbow Room Saloon,
don't like you drivin drunk
on a rainy night, I said.
Don't like it? he said
spit shinin the grip of his gun,
then find you another
mobile home to go live.
Don't make me feel like nothin,
I said, like I haven't been

for five years Harbor Inn waitressin
and bringin in half of our pay.
Women, he said, always forget
men got feelins too, ya know.
Come home sober the night before
won't bring me luck, he said,
could cause my boat
to get caught in a fog
with loon-call-echo the only thing
to guide me across the bay.
Women, he said
his wood-grip gun
smackin me across the face,
I oughta kill you if I can't
beat some sense into your head. . . .
And then, she said,
it was just like bein
a little girl back home
playin Gin Rummy with my brother:
When I'd win he'd come
at me with a hammer
and when I screamed
Ma'd slap my face, sayin,
you must have provoked him, Eudora.
But now, she said,
they've changed the rules around.
Next thing I knew
the cops was bendin over sayin,
better press charges, Eudora.
But all I could do was wonder
what gal in town
my husband'd go after next
and wonder where them cops was
back when I learned
that them who loved me, beat me.

Later, she said, I called
the Harbor Inn and told em,
fell on a beach rock
and can't be waitressin for a week,
I'm such a sight, I said.
Now, she said,
guess I know why salmon trollers
got women's names
painted on their sides.
No man's namesake'd sail
through gun-grip beatin waves
—not without buckin the blow
and bustin up at sea.
Didn't even wait, she said,
for my face to heal
before I crossed my name
off the side of that boat.
Couldn't sit and watch
them Alaska gales
batter the Eudora Dawn no more.
Painted my husband's name
below the bow, and now
I'm gonna watch how scared he gets
thinkin of gettin lost
in a walleyed fog and knowin
that them eerie loons'll
hush for once,
cause they'll be too busy divin
away from the bow of a boat
fool enough
to get itself named for a man.

I Canned Them Pears
and I Canned Them Pears

I used to wait under that tree
she said, for him.
I canned them pears
and I canned them pears
cause he loved em,
he loved that tree more'n anythin
—queen of fruits, he'd say.
I used to wait under that tree
for him, for the five o'clock whistle,
pickin pears
and when he died
I didn't can em up no more.
Never did like em much.
I give em to the neighbors
to my brother in Walla Walla
but he don't *do* for himself
and then they fall on the ground
and rot
and comes all them bees.
I got tired of waitin for the bees
to settle down
and tired of gettin stung
seein them pears
rot and him not here
to eat em.
Now people tellin me they're sorry
my pear tree died
real sorry
ol' tree like that, they say
big wind come an' split it down the middle,
tellin me they're sorry
cause them trees

leave such terrible scars
when the bulldozer come to pull em out.
I tied balin wire round the trunk, she said,
that fall after he died
and it took two maybe three years
for that tree to die.
I killed it, she said,
I killed it.
I canned them pears
and I canned them pears.

Hannah to Anthony,
Blowing Out the Flame Wick
of a Kerosene Lamp

Hannah on her front step
long chestnut hair
hanging down her back,
blowing his name,
Anthony, through the spaces
in her stump-fang teeth,
blowing his name out
like the flame wick
of a kerosene lamp,
the last vowel elongating
into the wind
of Hell Roaring Creek
into the smoke
of the salmon-cure
alderwood pit.
Calling his name
just like when she
threw his ashes into the tide,
"find ya a good-luck bone
before we throws em all in"
the other fishwives said
sifting through his bone dust
clanking black pieces
long as shark teeth together
in their palms. But
ain't no luck in that ash
ain't no luck in his name,
Hannah said rolling
his name out slow
like some witch-shaman word.

Anthony, five years drowned
and Hannah still digging
his bone ash like clams
out of Tidalflats mud—
his goldtoothed grin, chainsaw
face scarred and beard red
as squirrel-tail grass in August.
Hannah each year
before the salmon go running
visits the him
she finds in somebody else,
the him that would drive
stolen cars across Baja,
steal roofs off of barns
and ride railroads over
Great Northern Cascade
mountain pass trestles,
visits the Anthony who
left her so many times.
But now even his leavings are missed
like the noise of logging trucks
from the shut-down alderpulp mill.
So before the salmon go gathering,
before their silvery faces
find the creek
of their grandmother fish,
Hannah each year
digs him up again
remembering his hold
strong as a floodtide at Turnagain Bay,
remembering his anger
like a rainwind in autumn.
Hannah, her passion turning
to the wrath of Hell Roaring Creek,
turning to the cold of hoarfrost

on winterdead grass.
Ain't no luck in that ash
ain't no luck in his name,
Hannah says going
home to her front step,
calling his name, *Anthony*
elongating the last vowel
like the flame wick
of a kerosene lamp.
Anthony, pushing it through
the spaces in her stump-fang teeth.
A sword swallower I am, she says,
when I call out his name.
The last vowel so sharp
it cuts through the wind
and the alderwood trees.
A fire eater I am, she says,
blowing his name, *Anthony*
till the flame burns
her fingers, singes
the alderwood leaves.
Ain't no luck in that ash
ain't no luck in his name.

Hannah to Anthony,
blowing out the flame wick
of a kerosene lamp.

Like Geese They Come

to her back steps
weeds with names
she does not know
stealin her woodpile,
hid her hollyhock and rhubarb patch
last month.
The wash left on the line
for days
the grass too wet to mow
and them weeds leapin
for her gravensteins
up the trunk of her apple tree.
Cleft-leaved, some of em,
greener than the tide
and smellin strong
as fishgut rot and creosote,
weeds that by tomorrow
grown higher than her hair.
Like geese they come
tailwaggin hungry
to where she stacks
the cookstove wood
and her feedin em like birds
the cedar shakes torn
off the roof last March.
Says, them weeds guard
my woodpile'n apples
like no man ever did for me.
Not her Pa, husband dead
and all them men
like Roman candle leaves
in autumn overnight turned
gray as the sea dragged
and cannon shot for a week.
Better than any man,
she thinks with passion

dead as women whose stones
years of weeds have buried
over in the Baptist cemetery
—Ketura, his daughter,
Bathsheba, wife, consort of The Honorable—
women marked in death by names
of men who didn't do for em
what weeds can do.
Like geese they come
to her back step
watchin her axesplit wood
watchin her hang out the wash,
them keepin her apples'n kindlin
safe from neighborhands
and nightcaller crates.
Not many men been good to me
as weeds, she thinks,
feedin em piles
of last week's garbage
forgivin em for her hollyhock.
Whatcha want? she says,
their greeny tongues
lickin at her shoes,
whatcha want, doin for me
when I ain't done but harm
to you? Bendin her ear
into grass tall
as bed sheets on the line,
she makes out voices
of rootcrawl and seedrattle talk,
but like the raven callin out
the comin of the tide,
like fishfin thud and seagull nag,
like all them humanless soulless words,
the noisings of weeds
ain't writ in no books.
Whatcha want? she says,
whatcha want.

Glee Green's Sold-Off Old House

She hardly recognized
her blue hydrangea
all dried up, buried
under the woodpile and covered
with broken walkway cement;
the bush she'd pruned each fall
after the pom-pom flowers
lamplighted her kitchen
with lipstick chrysanthemums
arranged in *Mrs. Steward's*
liquid bluing bottles.
She hardly recognized
the window sashes
at the bottom of the heap,
pieces of her house
she'd painted redwood red
the year river-early-spring-thawing
and a Swinomish floodtide met
head-on
busting Main Street's sandbag dyke.
Now, putting her hand on a 4x4 post,
she lifts it up seeing
that the only thing living
under there other than sow bugs,
the only thing to grow up tall
through that pile of dislocated parts
is a horseradish leaf
—Gramma Green's quinsy cure,
same as asking for it
if ya don't plant one,
Gramma Green always said.
Touching the broad leaf's cleft,
Glee thinks of the root

growing underneath,
root like Gramma's
arthritic pale hand.
Then studying her new neighbor's
remodeled back porch,
glass in their roof,
a triangle window cut
in the north-facing wall;
what kind of people, she wonders
would kill a flower
in the full of its bloom?
But all the time
her neighbors never suspecting
underground a hand
growing and spreading,
a hand reuniting Glee Green
with the rest of her parts.

Chants

(1977–1981)

Long Time Ago When Words Were Magic

Long time ago when words were magic
when if you spoke them, things would happen,
Noise-Great-Beneath-the-Ground
voiced into the winter sky

words which made the northern lights
that at night are aqua blue.
Nowadays, put your ear to a marmot's hole
still hear that noise

down there rumbling as it walks around.
Or hear the seals in Glacier Bay
scratching at their icecrack breathing holes,
seals that once were fingers

of a screaming woman drowned
by men who held her under
during hunger-madness-time.
Gotta still take care with words nowadays

cause those seals are always telling
people-of-the-shade,
people who lived long time ago,
what the living're thinking and speaking.

Play mean tricks
those seals sometimes
hide the fish in Glacier Bay
make your boat come back without a catch

like those who died
in winter's hunger-madness-time.
People-of-the-shade,
see their tracks across the ice

see a wolf dead whose soul they've stolen.
People-of-the-shade, sometimes
feel them laying their hands on you
feel their fingers pull your sleeve

to those seals' icecrack breathing holes.
But people who lived long time ago
just always wanting you to listen:
Noise-Great-Beneath-the-Ground,

voice which made the northern lights
that at night are aqua blue,
voices of the seals
scratching at their icecrack breathing holes,

seals that once were fingers
of a screaming woman drowned
long time ago when words were magic
when if you spoke them, things would happen.

Song of the Undrowned

climb into the skin of a silver salmon
climb the kelp ladder down under the sea

singing with the great-noise-of-geese above her
she sits on a beach rock
mending fishnet, staring
into the brine-pewter bay,
between those sand bars
the blunt nose of a mud-dog shark,
beyond that conifer island
the wake of a blackfin whale,
and from the spruce
she watches land otters come hunting
bodies of the drowned to take
to their caves
dug in a hollow
of bonehills made
in old times
when a blackfin swam aground

and with them, across the beach
towards her comes walking
One-who-was-saved by the land otter people,
One wearing *his* face,
three years lost
when a seiner went under
—a winter too wet
for pitch sticks to smoke
the land otter's prey
out from their dens—
One-who-was-saved comes to her
lonely and pleading
as she runs to the waves
(where the drowned do not follow)

not letting his eyes
not letting his breath touch her face

a beach stone between her teeth
and swimming, she rolls with the swells
of the tide coming in,
swims like those who are looking
for the river mouth
of their grandmother fish,
singing with the great-noise-of-geese above her
song that keeps her safe
from the land otter power

climb into the skin of a silver salmon
climb the kelp ladder down under the sea

**Benediction for the
Salmon Spawning in Gray Wolf Creek**

they remember the creek of their foremothers
rise up
the steep cliffs
the rainforest
swimming against a glaciermelt
in Gray Wolf Creek
where I scrub camp pots
with wild moss
watching the salmon
down in their well

they remember the creek of their foremothers
rise up
looking like silver leaves
and sucker-fish
a dynasty of daughters
resting in the dark
of a fallen log
like stones

they remember the creek of their foremothers
rise up
the rocks of this creek
are slick for you,
touching a broodmare's hump
I ask, is this it?
here with the thimble berries
the cedar trees
the last stop
is this it?

they remember the creek of their foremothers
rise up
trudging on
past the trail's end
a bridge gone out
fish, we could mark the decades by you
rise up the white water
rise up the rain
rise up

*On the fishing boats in Alaska, when a sudden storm arises,
the older fishermen often chant to the weather; singing to the
saanah, the southeast autumn rain wind, and to Qa, the raven
demigod.*

Song of the Sitka Wind

Saanah, womanwind southeast wailing,
ptarmigan fly around and around
ptarmigan fly up crick and down
ptarmigan thirsty, so thirsty
ptarmigan hungry, so hungry

Saanah, womanwind southeast wailing
Raven *Qa*, Raven-at-the-head-of-the-Nass
give me your raven coat, your raven mask,
ptarmigan burrow head first in a snow hole
ptarmigan burrow head first in a snow hole

Saanah, womanwind southeast wailing,
hides the sun in a raven face
wraps the day in a raven skin, brings
Land-of-Long-Night to ptarmigan's house
Land-of-Long-Night to ptarmigan's house

Saanah, womanwind southeast wailing,
Qa in a rage puts out his raven neck
everyone guarding Spirit-of-the-Smoke-Hole
Qa, in a rage draws up his raven beak
everyone guarding Spirit-of-the-Smoke-Hole

Saanah, womanwind southeast wailing
no matter how long, no matter how hard
no one speaks against womanwind's song,
Raven *Qa*, Raven-at-the-head-of-the-Nass
give me your raven coat, your raven mask

Sila*

raven chatter and raven yell
raven strutting on the riverbank
trots along hunting salmon bones,
pearl necklace–like
fish spines come unstrung
when raven tosses discback moons
blacking out the copper sun,
beak dog-snouted, fish-hook sharp
raven digging in the ground
holes to hide the salmon bones

SING: *sila, sila*
sila, sila

tail thud and kick fin noise
salmon tacking into the mouth
of almost dried-up No Name Creek,
mute they walleye stare
the slate night sky
moving rockbound like lizards
instead of fish,
while windpruned cliffs
and windpruned spruce
echo body scream against the stones,
steely shining ragged skins
snag the stars as they shoot upstream,
raven chatter and raven yell
raven watching a thousand moons
fall into the face of the mouth
of almost dried-up No Name Creek

SING: *sila, sila*
sila, sila

tree rot red as rust and peat bogs
riding Saddle Mountain down
to Salmon Bay,
like fog the fish roll in
like fog they cannot be held
back from a reef of fins, rocktorn
their eyes pecked out
their eyes pecked out
raven chatter and raven yell
here, come here, fish
here the mountain bogs
here wet the color of rust
come here the red water
the rain, the rising mist
come here fog coming
here, come

SING: *sila*

*Alaskan weather spirit

Beneath the Pole of Proud Raven

She said, Creek Daughter
give me your gray gray hair,
creek daughter, give me
the glacier water,
—gray hair, cold water—
give me their child, creek daughter
give me the fish, creek daughter
give me your gray gray hair

She said, Fish
give me your silver skin, fish
give me your silver silver skin
give me your silver salmon skin
fish, give me your skin

She said, Loon
give me your noise, loon
give me your high pitched crazed call,
give me your loon-call echoing
off the island rocks, loon
give me your noise, loon
give me your noise

She said, Wolf
tired wolf, tired swimming wolf
give me your claws, tired wolf
give me your claws

She said, Crow
give me your coat, crow
give me your raven down coat
give me your coat like night,
crow, give me the night, crow
give me your coat

She said, Woman
give me the fog, woman
give me the fog, give me
the spruce-root hat where
you've hidden the fog
woman, give me the fog

She said, Coals
give me the fire spirit, coals
give me your pitch-stick smell,
give me your spruce-gum smoke
coals, give me the fire spirit

She said, Whale
give me your bones, blackfin
give me their slopes and hills,
bring me the mountains, whale
give me your bones

She said, Creek Daughter
give me your gray gray hair
give me the glacier water
She said, Fish
give me your silver silver skin
She said, Loon
give me your noise, loon
She said, Wolf
tired swimming wolf
give me your claws
She said, Crow
give me your coat like night
She said, Woman
give me the fog
She said, Coals
give me the fire spirit
She said, Whale
give me your bones, blackfin
bring me the mountains

She said,
I am the glacier
She said,
I am the fish
She said,
I am the loon
She said,
I am the wolf
She said,
I am the night
She said,
I am the fog
She said,
I am the fire
She said,
I am the mountain
She said,
I am the power
She said,
I am the earth
She said,

Beware

Letters

(1973–1976)

from *Letters from the Promise Land, Alaska*
and *The Clackamas*

The Aleutians

I read your old letters
the ones from Alaska
the ones from the boats
the purse seiners, the trawlers.
You say
you're waiting for crabbers
on their way back from Adak.
You talk about
getting on at the cannery
—it's king crab season,
boiler pots,
the two bad years.
Fish canneries
—PAN ALASKA—
factories using people up
like shoes.
You write
from a town out on the Aleutians
talking about the rubbish-littered shacks,
the trailers,
your bunkhouse
when the roof blew off
and there were just the sides
covered
with playboy pin-ups
men's magazines—
the smell of dirt,
smells of cigars
and women on the walls
advertised like "3 Musketeers"
to munch on
to fuck
to eat for breakfast.

It's the ambition,
the adventure you say
that drove you there,
living in the barracks
of an empty war naval station.
"Today, I walked on the beach,"
you wrote
"collecting seaweed.
The wind blows here
more than a hundred and thirty miles an hour,
the rain stings,
the ravens bark on the roadsides.
There are no trees on these islands
there are no women
there are no trees
and ravens bark
on the roadsides."

The Skin Business

I went into the mountains,
he wrote:
Here the islands rise
6,000 feet from the sea.
I looked down, into the ice.
Down on Unalaska, Captains Bay,
down into the growl of diesel generators
and men shooting seals
near the trawlers.
Fur's big business here
pelts going for a hundred dollars.
And then there's that fox,
the Red Aleut Fox
with a thick hennaed tail.
I saw her up there,
chased her into the hills,
through the shale,
up to where the diesels are silent.
I got close, so close,
he wrote
I could hear scratching
on the crusted ice.
I chased her for hours
just to hear the claws.
Red, hey Red,
you ain't easy, Fox
you ain't easy.
But then there's seal hunting
—we could be commercial hunters,
you and I.
It's big money,
I picked off five seals
just standing on the bow

of the *Olaf and John*.
And these hills,
these hills are fulla Red,
I chased her over the glaciers . . .
We could be hunters
you and I.
Big money, each shot,
each spring of a trap.
We could get close, so close,
we could hear Red,
we could hear claws
running
on the crusted ice.

The Men
After Crossing the Gulf from Kodiak

From Ketchikan to Dutch Harbor
lusting the money of the northlands
—tanner crab season,
the pipeline, the cold.
You say you baited halibut hooks
crossing the gulf from Kodiak.
You say you feel good today,
telling me how it is
with the men up there,
men walking the front street
of Dutch Harbor.
There's this instant,
you say,
a category
made at a glance,
made like an insurance policy, like a dog.
"I got him
and I got him," you say,
"but Lee?
Lee's a big man in the company."
And then there's this Eskimo Tommy,
a skinny five-footer,
thick lenses and bad hearing
and homesick for Bethel,
calling the Filipinos
at the cannery
half-breeds.
The men, flabby guts and fishbowl eyes,
breathing tobacco alcohol.
Breathing the knives, the booze,
the words,
the drunken screaming

of a bunkhouse fight.
The men, you say
two men meeting
on the front street
of Dutch Harbor,
the glance,
"I got him and I got him,
but Lee,
Lee's a big man in the company.
Put me down hard.
So I watch," you say,
"I watch,
lookin to change
the balance."

We Fish Our Lives Out

On the boats all day
drinking.
Eight fishermen
and a galley table,
cups, half-empty whiskey
tequila bottles,
cigarettes.
Talking up big bucks
with the cannery women.
A couple of days ago
the skipper of the *Sea Spray*
fell overboard and drowned,
two years back
six men never got from the Elbow Room
to their bunks.
All look the same,
these beaches,
flat
the sea,
a desert
no one learns to swim in
and maybe just one body washes
ashore.
We don't just talk fishing,
we fish,
fish all the trips we've ever been on.
Fish the world, do decades of fishing
in a whiskey bottle
at the galley table.
We fish our lives out,
drink
crash
wake up
leave at 6
drink
fish till dark.

We Run All Night

Left at midnight,
heavy weather.
The boat icing up, danger
big danger
bobbing, maybe going under.
But we start fishing before the light.
Pulling pots
heavy wind,
crab pots
iron
600 lbs,
big as two telephone booths.
We pull em up
full of tanner crabs
giant crabs with macabre crab faces.
Rip em out
fast
breaking legs
pinchers
still thrusting
food
to their mouths.
We run all night
sleep at 3
fish again at 6
breakfast, fish till dark.
My arms ache
no money
—fifteen wounds
healing
in my hands.

Notes on a Life

(1973–1975)

from *This House That Rocks with Every Truck on the Road*

Desperado

Even in my dreams
I wait for you
      —a smile
sliding through the tall grass,
through the corn.
The rocks have taught me
this waiting,
I have their persistence
scratching, knocking
at the slick doors
that keep you in.
I long for you,
Desperado,
the kiss, the white
teeth of passion,
to lie with you
watching
for that hell in your eye.
It's the death wish within you
that draws me so near,
beyond the sting of your skin,
closer
to the edge of you.
Let me see,
let me in.
I have to touch
the things
that will never be mine.

The Codling Moth

A white moon,
and his head in my arms.
Blond lashes wing
like moths
against my skin.
White moths
and the apple trees,
winesaps,
yellow delicious,
fruitpickers on the road
hitching a ride to Wenatchee.
Gonna pick the culls,
listen to the farmers' talk,
co-op men saying
that jobbers don't want
hail marks and frost pocks.
Saying ya gotta insure the crop
against the codling moth,
against the cull;
the housewives' disgust.
The moths,
ya trap em in cans.
The blond wings that rustle my skin,
trap em in cans.
Cans of poisoned pheromone.
Poison pussy,
synthesized and bottled
by a smartass college kid
who won a prize for it,
won a prize from the insurance companies,
the absentee landowners.
Female incense
canned-up in quart jars,

canned like quince jelly
trapping the blond lashes
against my skin.
Trapping the codling moth
on my shoulders,
my arms,
with that same quince jelly,
that same sweet lie
that holds me
still.

Tastes Like Chicken

I have driven the deserts,
I said.
I have driven them alone,
across the Cascades
across Lake Chelan
into the dry heat
into the Desert, the East.
That wild asparagus by the roadside
and the rattlesnakes
I wanted for dinner;
"Tastes like chicken,"
everybody said.
"Tastes like chicken
and if yr careful
could be twice's cheap."
I meant to run one down
on the road back to Omak
on the road across the reservation
to Big Goose Lake.
A snake with seven rattles
          —I chased her from beneath
the hot tires of my truck.
Chased her across the graveled road
back to the dry grass
back to the magpies
and the dust.
Snake.
You high-ass, high-cunt
thin-legged
high-stepping
Snake.
You taste like chicken!
You and your long back bones

your blond-bellied tease,
c'mon, Miz Snake,
bite.
Teach me the sting.
I know that energy
the rage,
slipping beneath the tar weed,
the *S* ribbon in the dust
of your swan-necked retreat.
I know it all,
all except
for the sweet sure bite
and the skill.

Angelica

2:00 A.M.,
reeling lights in the street.
Volunteer firemen
searching the hill, the rocks.
They knock at the neighbors'
asking questions.
They say they are looking
for a young child,
a little girl.
And what do I say
when they stop at my door?
       —In the early evening
I pulled the onions,
braiding the stems into chains.
I did not see her stop
by the back shed,
standing akimbo,
eating the squash blossoms.
I did not see her
in the barn
as I caught the banties,
grasping the legs,
pushing each in a sack.
But no one talks
of a "victim."
They only say that the lobelia
is so blue
even in the night.
Shall I tell them?
Shall I say
that there are knots in her hair,
that she runs with the wild dogs
where the tops blew out

of the eagle trees?
That afternoon, the Indian tidelands.
Was it the clam flesh
that has left me sick?
Was it the taste of her? . . .
She has taken the air
to those secret oyster beds,
we pried them from the rocks
she and I,
shells razor edged.
We ate them raw.
We ate them alive.

All the Naked Fields

All around me
there were the white mountains,
the white mountains,
the corn,
and the sea.
Rural towns,
farmers, fishermen.
I have looked for my face
among them
        —but there is only the click
of their teeth,
the orange of calendula,
potato harvesters,
miles of them, locusts.
These people
do not notice
that I am gone
beneath the skin.
They whisper that
it's an old man
from Methow
axing the sunflowers
leaving them out to dry.
No one says the word,
no one guesses
that I have come
to eat the grass,
the seed for sugar beet.
I have eaten them all
and my gums bleed
from the stones.
My hair blows
in the dry silt-loam,

rolling with the apples,
walking slow.
I shall not stay long,
I say
to the wild grape,
to the dust on the dark weeds.
Kiss me good-bye.

Talking That Talk

(1975–1979)

Glitter Box

What do these men really want
I said.
What they really want
is some hassle-free woman.
What they're looking for,
I said,
is no depressions,
light to medium moods
and not too often.
What they really want
in a woman
is a glitter box,
Carmen Miranda fruits
in a gypsy skirt.
But underneath,
under the dress,
the frilly red French bikini
panties and bra,
underneath
it had better be mama,
I said.
It had better be mama
and not any flaming parrot.
No bedroom in 19th-century
Mediterranean brothel decor.
Under all that mascara
it had better be mama
sitting up straight
on a dentist office Sears-Roebuck
couch
reading *Redbook*,
canning-up

sweet-sour cantaloupe pickles
for a treat.
It had better be warm and mama
under there, I said.
And that's the catch,
the terrible trick;
that's the myth of the mishuguna,
the crazy lady.
Women get used to being the glitter
and then the mama underneath.
They get used to that,
they get to know that
as the only way
of getting by.

Don't Cheapen Yourself

You look sleazy tonight,
ma said.
Cheap, I said,
I'm doin cheap.
You got any idea
how much it costs
to do cheap these days?
To do gold City of Paris
three-inch platform sandals
and this I. Magnin snake dress?
I'm doin cheap.
You look like a bird, she said,
a Halloween bird with red waxed lips.
     —In high school
you could either do cheap or Shakespeare,
college prep or a pointy bra,
ratting a bubble haircut
with a toilet brush.
I was not allowed to do high school cheap,
I did blazers and wool skirts
from the Junior League thrift shop.
In high school it was
don't walk in the middle of
Richie, Leelee, and the baby,
you might come between them.
You look like a skag
wearin that black-eyed makeup,
people are gonna think you're cheap.
While I poured red food dye
on my hair
to match my filly's tail for the rodeo,
ma beat her head against the wall,
she said

trying to make me nice.
I tried real hard,
but the loggers, the Navy guys,
they always hit on me.
Cause you're an easy mark, ma said.
And I played guilty,
I played guilty every time.
But now, I said,
now I'm doin cheap.

Fix Me a Salami Sandwich,
He Said

Fix me a salami sandwich,
he said,
I don't wanna fix it myself
if you love me
you'll fix me a sandwich
you have to help me, he said,
you have to take care of me
sometimes,
he said,
I need mothering
I need you to tell me
you love me
I need to hear you say it
I need you to sleep with me
I need you to fuck me
I need you to be on top
when we fuck
what time is it?
where's those phone numbers
that green matchbook with the raised
gold lettering
with the phone numbers
on the inside
I put it right here
I'm hungry
I haven't had time to get to the grocery
I need comforting
I need a ride to the corner
let's have coffee together for once,
he said,
you make coffee,
he said,

I don't like these raw vegetables
I don't like this smelly cheese
it smells like cunt,
he said,
it smells like I have pussy
all over my fingers
you don't take care of me,
he said,
I have needs,
he said,
I have certain needs
and you don't do "Mommy"
very well, he said,
you don't do "Mommy"
at all, he said.

Tight Denim Jeans

I'd never wear a girdle, she said,
just medieval throwbacks
to whale baleen brassieres'n
lace-up waist confiner corsets.
We burned em in the sixties,
girdles, she said walking
into Bloomingdales, grabbing
a pair of cigarette-legged
tight denim jeans off the rack.
Hoisting them up to her hips,
how do ya get em on? she said,
have surgery, take steam baths,
slimnastic classes'n Dr. Nazi's
dietclinic fatshots for a month?
These aren't jeans for goin
to lunch in, she said trying
to do up the snap, these
aren't even jeans
for eatin an hour
before ya put em on, just
for standin up in without
your hands in the pockets,
there's not even room
in here for my underpants.
One hour later she returns
to the store for a new zipper,
front snap, and the side seams
restitched. These're jeans
for washin in cold water only
then wearin round the house
til they dry on yr shape,

put em in a clothes dryer,
she said, and you'll get
all pinch bruised
round the crotch'n
your stomach covered
with red streak marks
cross the front.

We burned em in the sixties,
girdles, she said.

And That's a Big Ten-Four

for Richard Katz

Breaker, one seven
anyone out there lonely?
Anyone know the twenty
of the Bull Frog Saloon?
It's wall-to-wall smokies
all the way to Fresno
so keep it under the double nickel.
Breaker, you got your two-way on?
Come On
I gotta get this Del Monte tomato rig
to the slab by mornin
and all that's on the AM
is some cowboy
singin "Johnny Generator"
all the way up the Altamont grade.
Breaker
anyone know where I can get a joe-dog
for my two axle?
Anyone out there lonely?
My heater's busted
and it's colder
than a brass brassiere in here.
Come On, Breaker
this is your *Rubber Band Man*
what's your handle?
Even Billy Carter's got a handle
calls himself *Cast Iron.*
Anybody out there got a copy?
Jezebel, Flyin Hawaiian,
California Bull Shipper?
Anyone out there lonely?
Well guess I'll catch you all on the flip
Rodger D
and that's a big ten-four.

**Lady in a Hundred Dollar Car
One Night on the Side of the Road**

So I says to this guy,
Arny, show me where to put
the transmission fluid in,
and he wants to know if
my husband bought me
the old Chevy cause
I kept strippin the gears
and burnin out the clutch.
I ain't got no husband,
I says liftin up the hood,
and maybe you could
just show me where
to put the tranny fluid in.
No, I ain't got no flashlight
I says and he whips out
a boxa match sticks
tellin me he's gotta be
real careful about
carburetor hydrogen gas.
Just one false move, he says,
poof, no more Arny, see
whatta favor I'm doin for you?
No more my car, I says.
Just a few more matches, he says,
it's gotta be under there
in all them wires somewhere.
Careful, I says, maybe
you shouldn't go stickin
your hand down into the dash
and disconnectin the ignition.
Besides, I don't gotta know
tonight where to put

the tranny fluid in, I says,
this car's been runnin 16 years
it can wait until mornin.
Trust me lady, he says,
this's really got my goat.
Careful of that spark plug wire,
I says. Sorry about that, he says.
Yeah, I says, guess it'll run
just as good on seven, why not?
there's no hills around here.
Let's turn on the headlights,
I says, and look in the manual
and he says, see here it tells ya
to keep the fluid level
just below the add-a-quart line.
That's the powersteerin lubrication,
I says, and he says, trust me
it's gotta be under there
in all them wires somewhere.
Careful of that terminal, I says
and he says, ok, ok, we can always
hook up the ignition again,
just tell me where the starter
motor is and I says, I don't know
where the starter motor is,
I don't even know
where the tranny fluid goes in,
but it's ok, I says, this car's
been runnin 16 years.
What'd ya mean ya don't know
where the starter motor is?
he says, I thought ya were
the kinda woman who knew
about cars. Gimme another match,
he says, it's really got my goat,

he says, I'm gonna find it
if I gotta tear out every one
of them friggin wires. But
what about carburetor hydrogen gas
and, poof, no more Arny? I says
and he says, trust me lady,
just gimme another match,
what d'ya think I am
stupid or somethin?

**What D'ya Get When Ya Cross
a Gynecologist with a Xerox Machine?**

Put the flat tire on the table,
he says; jacks me open
spotlights, probing,
staring down my turkey hole.
There's blood in here! he shrieks,
it's blood, it's a mess,
it's another smelly twat;
there's boxes all over your room.
Yeah, I said, boxes,
play clothes here
and school clothes there
in the boxes between ma's bed
and the television.
Three to five years of garbage in here,
he says, stacks of laundry, sheets, shopping carts.
What are the symptoms?
Where does it hurt?
It's those birdcalls again, I said.
They come all the time.
Can you hear them?
It's a hoot, a caw,
it's a Martinique yellow thrush.
I could teach you . . .
Not me, not this boy,
motherhood, he said,
reproduce yourself,
see you with a new face on,
in several poses,
it'll give you a lift.
Sounds like a Xerox machine, I said,
an IBM shooting white-sheeted sperm.
Xerox, I said.

It's a mess in here, he said,
piles of garbage,
playpens, strollers;
looks like someone got a divorce,
moved away and left it all.
And all these old letters, he said.
Letters from mama, I said.
Reproduce, he said.
Here, let's practice;
breathe in, breathe slow, take a letter:
Dear Son,
Why do you always have to hurt and kill?
Just be yourself.
I am doing O.K.
Love, ma, he said.

Laments

(1975–1977)

from *The Clackamas*

Throw em All Back

1.
He's dead, they said,
filled this can with charcoal
trying to keep warm.
The camper
the state park at Vantage
dead.
Ya got the wrong guy, I said,
that's some other body
an avalanche,
a boat wreck, maybe
when the deadeye radar's
gone in the fog
but not quiet
not from charcoal briquettes
and trying to stay warm.

Or maybe he'll just call
saying it's all a joke
that bright face knocking at the door
that *schmerk*
handing me an architecturally dried fish
saying "here, Snail,
I brought you a little present.
It was a joke
a calculated emotional experience,
a transgression of taste
a little fun
now we'll go to North Beach
buy you a dress."
All those presents from Alaska
a taxidermied crab

an octopus beak
a joke.
It's a joke, I said.

2.

But they burnt you up
without me, didn't even write
the relatives
the names you couldn't remember.
Now I lay on my bed
with an empty list
of all the things I wouldn't do
to bring you back to me.
Your friends,
we spent a week
looking for what was left.
We needed a body
for the proof,
but all there is
is your empty truck
the cold wood stove
the hungry cat.
He's gone, I said,
maybe at the tavern
I don't know
—running through the mustard fields
gone to play with my childhood pets
my guinea pig
my Pola dog.
Gone
gone to ash.

3.

Yeah, I said,
I left him

so he couldn't leave me anymore
so he couldn't run off
to the lure of Alaska
to conquer the winds of atom bomb tests
and the ice,
so he couldn't hurt me.
    You couldn't
    anymore
    but even then
    you found a way.
    You did it up for keeps
    left me again
    the same pain
    bang
    bang
    you're dead, they said.
And this time
there's no salmon trawler
no seiner, nowhere on earth
I can send these letters to.

4.

His Ma says
he died of his own wrong life,
deserting the student loans
running out
drinking wine.
Says I left
made him so unhappy
that last Christmas of his life.
Yeah, I said,
I was afraid,
spent a year on the couch
trying to figure it out.
Was it death, that energy

that light in his eye?
Was it me?
I could be dead, I said.
     But they forgot,
     those shrinks,
     they forgot to say
     that leaving you
     wouldn't kill the love
     wouldn't stop you
     wouldn't put the death-light out.
I left, I said,
that house, that smiling face
clear as a poppy
the day he went to swim
in the outgoing tide
drunk on homebrew
came home shaking, almost drowned.
Left, left that smile
to haunt me
to light my dreams.
     Who, who was it
     that was gunning for you?
     Who was it
     you were trying to kill?

5.

     Was it your mother in me?
The relatives,
sad hags
had a good laugh on me.
But I have his face, I say,
his hand on my shoulder
the kick from behind,
since the day we met
I do the things I do

with his good wishes.
And if they try to steal
his house from me
I'll burn it down
I'll burn it
to the sound of his drunken laughter
I'll burn it
the way they burnt him
the way they burnt the only proof
I'll burn it down, I say.
    You know what crimes of passion
    are for.

6.

Dear Girl,
they write.
Received the photographs
you must have known
they would sadden us
people like you
bring out the worst
in this child's eye.
Wish you could have seen him
lying on deep red
edged with white
lilies
his last service
a blue shirt at his throat
his lovely auburn hair.

Dear Girl,
ask God to destroy the hate
help
to remember
to cherish
the love you once had.

It's the alcohol that's made all this—
for all of you
find ways to stop
the others
from turning
into ash.
Ask God for help.
Signed, lovingly
his cousin
his mother.

7.

We fought over you
when you were alive
and now that you're dead
we fight over your old auto parts
your skillsaws
your vacant lot out on the slough.
"Worth a thousand bucks
at least," they said.
But I gave em all away,
the tools
the electric drills
the one you zapped
through your thumb
on purpose,
the hole, you said,
would release the blood
the pain
the hammer-smashed nail.
Gave em all away
to the friends
the girl you'd met last month,
gave em to that face that was my face
the braids

I'd cut last year
to Cassandra
whose letters were my letters
coming back
unopened,
hitching across the mountains
baggy Levis, Goodwill boots
down to the orchard to meet you
to knock at your door—
he's dead, they said.
To my own nightmare,
I gave em all away.

8.

Dear husband,
I loved you and you left
so many damned times,
left me here
to face these brutes
the real estate agents
the finance companies
the relatives, the courts.
My dresser mirror is covered
with your photos
postcards of you
from Chelan, Unalaska, Michoacan.
And there's nowhere on earth
I can send these letters to
no fishing trawler
on the waves of grief
on the sea of the dead—
there are no tides
no telling when
the crash comes above my head.
We fished the seas out

you and I
the one the other
the rudder the sail.
How many, how many fish
have these hands caught?
To see your smile
and those calloused thumbs
the wounds healing
in your palms
to run them across my face
snag my cheek
one last time.
How many?
The urn, the ash
"throw em to the four winds"
you said,
"throw em to the fish
the waves, shit baby
I don't care, goddamn it"
you said.
"Throw em all back."

Five Eagles Watched

Poem for Dead Husband

1.
Me and you
we had it all
all the neuroses
German parents
obsessed
with poverty
and good taste
would allow.
The getting
the working three jobs
saving up years
like canned peaches.
On the road
moving through
a thousand miles
of goat hovel
shanties
and stillborn dreams,
we had it all.

2.
Lookalikes
with our slanty-eyed
Hun mamas.
Me playing big sister
got you to the dentist on time,
you played the daddy
helping me off the roof
patching shingles
the day
five eagles

watched
wordless
from a dead-topped spruce.

3.

I should write you
that the corn came up
in December,
write you
my last night's dream:
You in the kitchen
at a faculty party
cutting onions
on my pig board.
Me saying
come back
please
come back
and you
—smiling face—
No, baby,
—laugh—
I ain't never
I ain't never
comin back.
I should write you that.

4.

What about the gossip
saying you done yourself in
—but I know.
I know the day you died
you did things
you'd never do.
You weren't there
alone,

somebody else
got you in that hole.
Trouble is
I don't know where to start,
some of them had you there
for thirty years
and some
some just hit on you
by accident.

5.

I write the news
over and over
—on November 9th
working near Lake Chelan . . .
he always spoke so well of you.
Over and over
a naughty school girl
given a hundred sentences
"I will not chew gum in class"
"I will not chew gum in class"
cause this would make me a better girl.
His friends saying they're sorry
but no matter how many times
I write this letter
they'll never think
I'm good.

6.

That German heritage
blue eyes
and a young grave
I told you
I told everyone
and nobody listened.
So how come

it's just me
yelling *murder?*
 Those Germans
driving stakes
through the blond faces
of their children,
the wars
the wars
that killed you
before you were born.
The smell of guns
fallen logs
on a flatcar
steel tracks
sliding knives
through the moon.
It's murder, I say,
cleaning my rifle
the one you used
to hunt deer, you said.
Your face
Hugo Blanco
your face is buried
all over Germany.
I'll get em, I say,
but how come
how come it's just me
yelling *murder.*

7.

Your name
your name
taught me
the hammer
the nail

catspaw pulling
cedar sliding
off the shed.
Your name
wailing
on the metal roof
—the one we stole
off the barn
by the slough.
Your name
your name
rolling at the end
of the tide
forever prevailing.
Listen.

Envoi

(1976–1979)

The Clackamas

White rocks
lined with cottonwood
and leaves the underside
like quarters chiming
in the pocket of my
borrowed-from-my-best-friend
summer dress.
Miles of river
lined in dead-car skeletons,
"Cross my palm"
says the gypsy lady sign
at the Carver Bridge
—Cross my heart, sweet river
shrunken by summers
almost gone.
I turn
find you
not beside me
like the buildings
of my childhood
torn down.

The Suitcase

Unopened in ten years
kept like an old home movie,
picture of a milltown girl
with her secondhand
cowhide suitcase

Sent off with goodbye words
hurriedly mouthed
through a Greyhound
mud-and-dust covered
window

The suitcase filled
with schoolgirl poems
carted dormitory to attic,
poems with the "s" in "she"
left out and red letter A-ed
at the top

Packed between the one white blouse
yellow under the arms,
a sanitary napkin belt, and
a pair of fishnet nylons
snagged by her first husband's
lug-soled boot

Inside the satin pockets
her notes on Blake and Frost,
the suitcase of a girl
who wanted to write poetry
like Grand Ol' Opry singing

Inside the pockets
where she hid her stories
of milltown wives
saving Green Stamps
saving plastic bags

to crochet into doormats,
stories still bearing
the red capital "E"
"Embarrassing and learn the difference
between literature and personal life"

Among the chain-stitched patches
on her crazy-quilt skirt,
in her collection
of psychedelic Indian jewelry,
where are the clues to say
that whatever "great things are done
when men and mountains meet,"
these remnants of her are here
and the dead husband isn't?

A bit of seam binding
a button found on the street,
the suitcase of a girl
who did not yet know
that when it was her turn
to stand behind the podium,
it would not be
these men's words
but her own
she would speak

This heap of papers and
flower-child fringe
so guarded of the telling
that, unlike a snowy-haired poet
who addressed audiences of presidents,
for this milltown girl
and her cowhide suitcase
there would not be
a highway untraveled,
there would not be
two roads to choose from

Laundry

for Anna

A fine arts degree in laundry?
you're nuts, they said . . .
but I'm haunted, she said,
out my window
the labor of the world
drying in the sun.
The white sheets of Tehran
the yashmaks
spinnakers sailing open mast
into the words of women washing
    laundry hung.
Haunted, she said,
by milltown women
pinning pillowcases
with metal-sprung clothespins
and bits of paper bag
in winter
so they don't rust through the line.
Haunted by the pulley squeak
    laundry hung
punctuated in cashmere
sweaters shrunk to fit
marilyn monroe style
and rows of pantyhose.
Words on the page
laundry on the line
cross stitched
through the back yards
by the railroad track,
    laundry hung.
Study the laundry of the world,
she said,

fill the museum of modern art
in new york city with clothesline,
red bandanna cowboy shirts
and bo-peep night gowns,
their shape's fresh smell
their dark lives on the wall,
the language of the world
strung up to dry,
sounds of a thousand years
of women washing
    laundry hung.

Vera on the BART Train

In her fifties
in winged rhinestone bifocals
and a suitcase like the one
my childhood 78 speed record player
lived in,
Vera, it says in gold letters
by the handle,
is that really your name?
In a stretch-and-sew polyester coat
that doesn't hide the white uniform
the wide scuffs on your white shoes,
you nod out and don't notice me
staring up the crack between your legs.
Vera, I make up biographies for you
—born Sabetha, Kansas, 1919
—born Spokane, Washington, 1924.
Vera denying chapped cleaning lady knees
in a new pair of pantyhose
denying tiredness
in white gloves and a suitcase
ready for domestic assignments.
Vera from a ramshackle house on
West 23rd Street
the sweet-smelling porch vine
broken under a salesman's shoe
hasn't bloomed since you left.
Vera, scrubbing the painted linoleum
of rented summer houses
cleaning off flies
stuck to bathroom walls
the dirt of a thousand fingers
crying "Vera
take my glass, my shoes."

Vera, nodding out to the far-off slam
of some back screen door,
riding away to clean
the vacant windows of a summer cottage
where children
light fires in the unmown grass.
Vera, that space between your legs
our secret place
a trunk left locked in the attic
a room Miss Lady never found.
Vera, if you can hear me
if you can read my thoughts
a glance, a sign,
tell me there is something
I might write
that could begin to avenge this, Vera.
Vera, woman like a house let out.

Lips

for Janan at 15

I

This year
at high school
if ya wanna be in
with the preppy icks
ya gotta wear
white loafers
and a lacrosse t-shirt.
Them sayin I can't wear red
cause I look Puerto Rican,
them askin how come
my Pa's Arabic
and he ain't rich,
ya just can't win
with those preppy icks.
Know what they do?
They all get together
and pair off, makin a pact
like who's goin steady
with who
tryin to make
the rest of us
believe it.
So how come
they think I'd
go out
with one of them?
But what I really wanna know is,
do things get better
when ya get grown up?

II
Just twenty-one
draggin the strip
with pretty boys
in hopped-up, 57 Chevys
passin the coke'n Bacardi.
Parkin out on the levee
in a corn field
with some hungry-eyed cowboy,
prayin that
he'll like me,
he'll like me.
And still wonderin
how old ya gotta be
before things get better.
How old ya gotta be
before some punk cop
stops waitin til
ya got everything off
before he pokes his high powered
flashlight into the back seat
askin for I.D.
when I can't even find
my panties
—the ones I'm old enough
to wear especially
for takin off—
askin for I.D.
when I know damn well
that light is reflectin
every one of those lines
across my swing-shift
cannery worker's face.

III

Thirty,
both of us
nervous and rusty,
haven't done it
with someone new
in a parked car
for years.
Both of us
living like
rented houses
borrowing our bodies back
for the night,
borrowing
from the husbands
and ex-wives
the lovers
whose nightmares
have become our own,
because we love them
we love them
and this rum'n coke
doesn't have the kick
it did before.
Both of us
sitting like trophies
on the hood
of some vintage
refurbished Chevrolet,
remembering when we parked
in a cornfield
escaping the lips
of our parents,
the mother who told us

how to feel,
the father
who never was there.
Two white-teethed roses
looking for something
in each other's arms
in the pants
of our pegged, cigarette-legged
shrunk-to-fit Levis.
And still so scared
we're gonna blow it
even though
we're only borrowed
for the night.

     IV

Later
watching a sunset of lips,
you say
you wanna kill
your ex-lover
and I say
I've been dead inside
for years.
Our arms fall
around each other
like corn silk
and we drown
in the water
of each other's mouths.
Lips,
those lips
that brought us here,
those lips that once

we stayed out late
in parked cars
to escape.
Lips are all I have left
of those days,
lips

I give you my lips.